THE IRISH HERITAGE

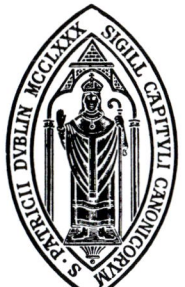

St Patrick's Cathedral

by Victor Jackson

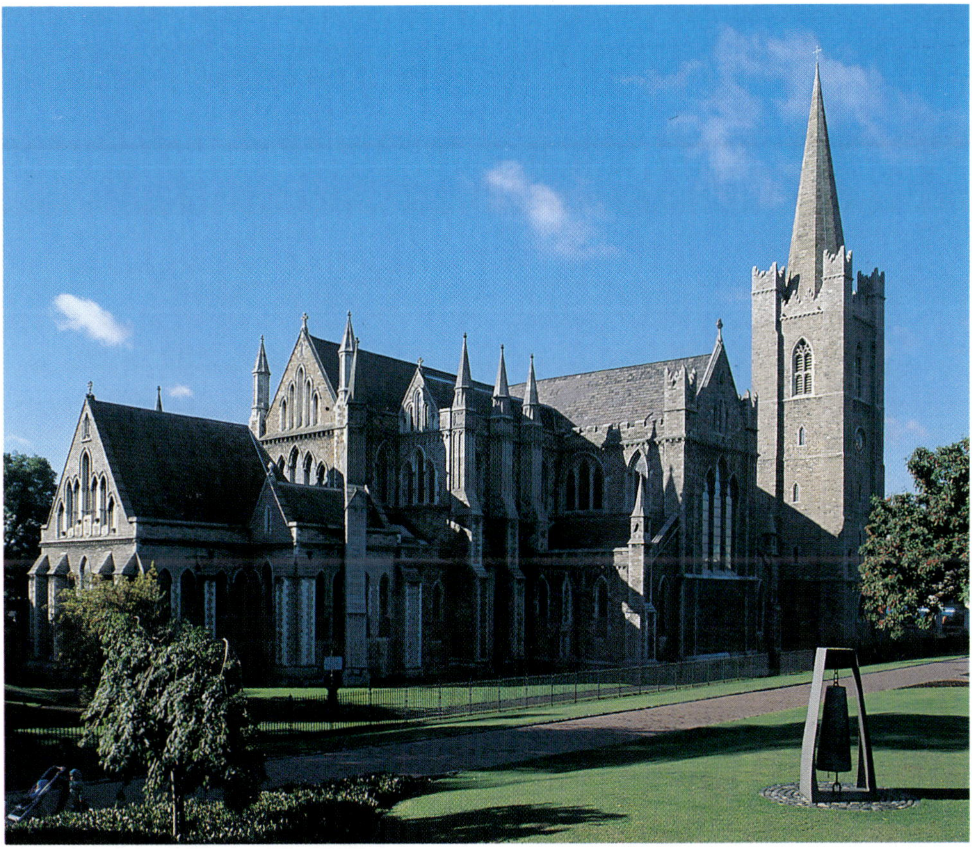

![Cathedral from St Patrick's Park]

1 The cathedral from St Patrick's Park

Little is known of the early life of St Patrick, the patron saint of Ireland. In his writings he provides a few details of his boyhood, but gives no information on the place and year of his birth, which is thought to have been on the west coast of Cumbria some time between AD 370 and 380. His father was Calpurnius, a deacon, and his grandfather, Potitus, was a presbyter.

At the age of about sixteen, when his father was living at a place called Bannaven Taburniae, Patrick was taken captive by raiders and brought to County Antrim in Ireland, where he served as a slave for six years. One night in his sleep he heard a voice which told him that a ship was ready and, accepting this as a message from God, he escaped, found the ship and sailed to Gaul. After many years of study he was ordained and later became a bishop. Again he saw a vision and heard voices coming, as he felt, from Ireland which said, 'We beseech thee, holy youth, to come and walk among us once more.' Being convinced that this was another sacred message, he sailed for Ireland about the year 432.

He landed near the town of Wicklow and from thence proceeded northwards along the coast, touching at Inis Patrick near Skerries, Carlingford Bay and finally landing at Strangford Lough. Here he converted and baptised a chieftain named Dichu who granted him the plot of land on which they were standing, called Saul or Sabhall, meaning a barn, and on the site of this barn St Patrick erected a church. He decided to visit his old master, Milchu, in Antrim, but Milchu dreaded that his former slave would exercise on him some evil influence and erected a funeral pile on which he burnt himself to death. St Patrick then travelled to Tara, in Meath, a centre of Irish paganism, and was successful in converting the king, Laoghaire. After seven years at Connaught he went to Ulster, where he founded the primatial See of Armagh in the year 445. He is known to have passed through the province of Leinster on his way to Munster, where he spent a further seven years, and during his travels he founded many churches. When he felt that his end was drawing near, he made his way back to Strangford Lough and, probably in the year 461, he died beside his church at Saul on 17 March, which became known as St Patrick's Day.

Just outside the walls of the old city of Dublin, to the south, stands the Collegiate and Cathedral Church of St Patrick on a site of great antiquity. According to ancient writings, St Patrick baptised a number of his converts at a well on one of his visits to Dublin and some time later a small wooden church was erected close by. Certainly local tradition in the twelfth century associated the name of St Patrick with a church built beside a sacred well. The site was most unsuitable as it was between two branches of the River Poddle, a small river which flows from the Dublin hills north-eastwards to join the Liffey. The well of St Patrick appears to have flourished until the late sixteenth century. Its site was rediscovered during excavations in 1901, when old houses were demolished and the present park beside the cathedral was being laid out. A stone slab (**2**), covering the remains of the ancient well, was unearthed, and is now preserved in the north-west end of the cathedral.

In the old Irish settlement of Dublin were four churches of Celtic foundation, St Bride's, St Michael-le-Pole, St Kevin's and St Patrick's, but following the Danish influence more and more churches were established as the population grew and the city developed. When Archbishop Laurence O'Toole died in 1180, the Anglo-Norman invasion was already well under way and the foreigners were firmly established in Dublin. King Henry II was very anxious to exert his influence over the Irish Church, so the rather untimely death of O'Toole was an opportunity for

2 St Patrick's Well stone

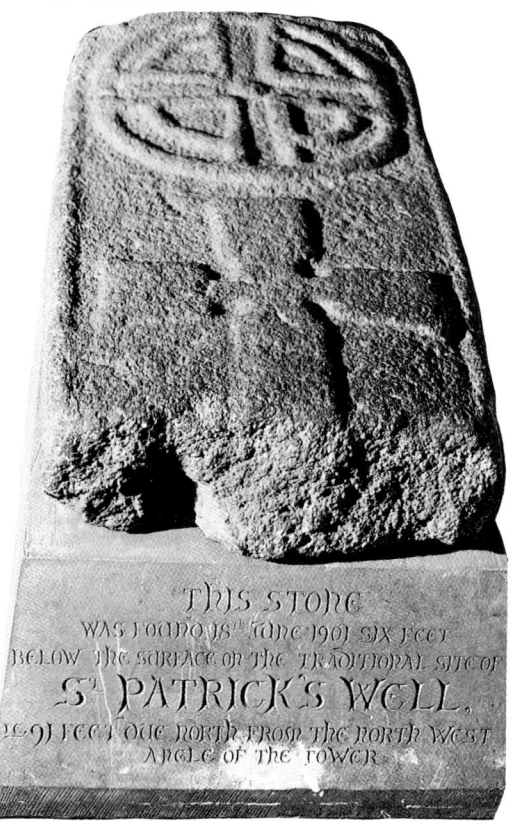

3 The choir and sanctuary

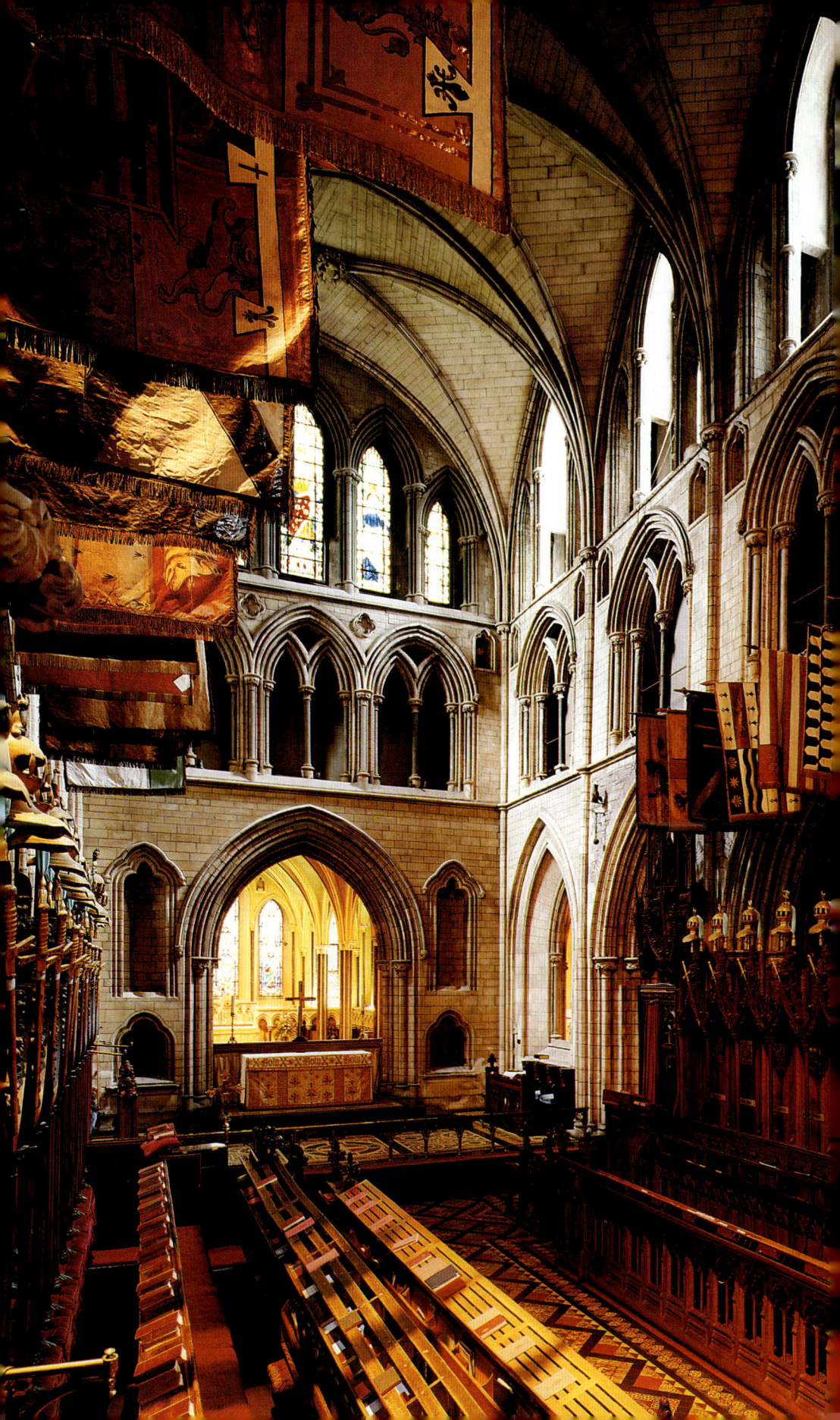

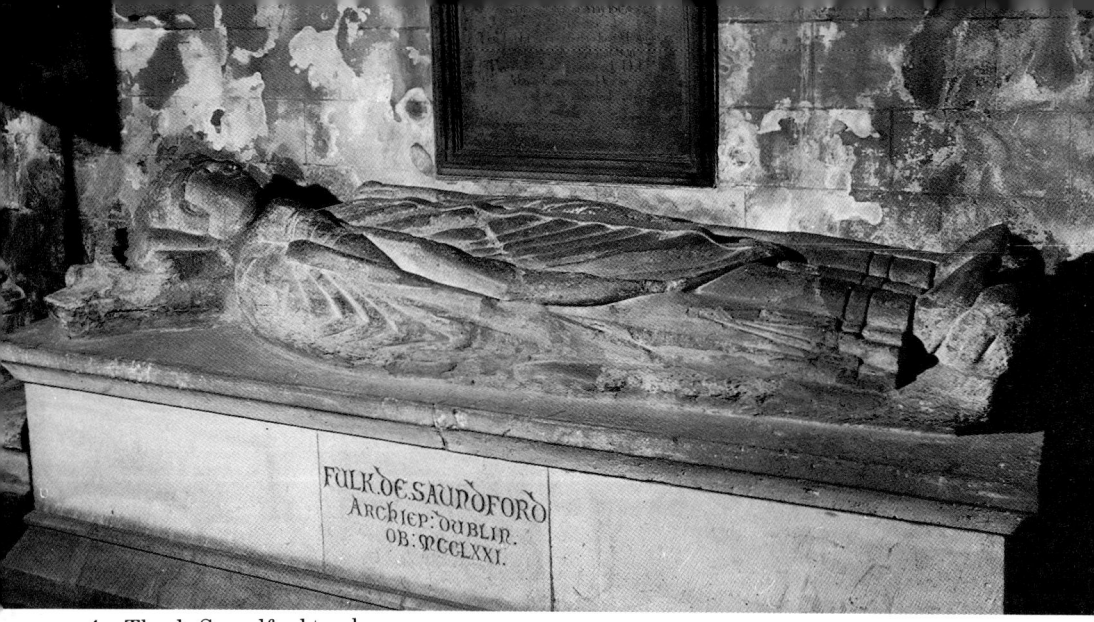

4 The de Saundford tomb

him to appoint one of his most trusted followers. John Comyn was a Benedictine monk from Evesham and had a wide reputation as a learned judge, an able diplomat and a brilliant administrator. Although enthroned as archbishop in England in 1181, he did not land in Ireland until 1184 when his first duty was to make plans for the forthcoming visit of Prince John in the following year.

Although Prince John's visit was hardly a success, he did make a number of important grants to John Comyn in order to enlarge and enrich the See of Dublin. When Prince John had departed, Comyn lost no time in imposing his influence and in carrying out the king's wishes to reorganise where possible the Irish Church, but he was disturbed by the Priory of Christ Church and the fact that he had to reside in a palace beside it. Christ Church Cathedral had been founded in the previous century with a secular organisation but Laurence O'Toole, following his appointment to the See of Dublin in 1162, had changed the constitution to the regular Order of Arrosian Canons. As the Normans were opposed to regular and monastic orders, Comyn found the organisation at Christ Church distasteful, but he was loathe to displease the local people by altering its character. He refused, however, to live in the palace, where he would be subject to the jurisdiction of the City Provosts, so he decided to erect a church and a palace outside the city walls on his own domain.

As archbishop, Comyn owned extensive lands north and south of the city, including the ground on which stood the old church of St Patrick. This church, beside the sacred well, he rebuilt 'in hewn stone in the form of a cross, right goodly to be seen with fair embowed works, fine pavements and an arched roof overhead with stonework' and the old name, so much venerated, he retained. Concerned about the lack of education and culture of the Irish people, he made his church collegiate, prebendal and secular, and for the support of the prebendaries, of whom there were thirteen originally, he granted them the lands and revenues from a number of his estates. Certain privileges were given to the prebendaries, and in addition to their clerical and teaching duties they were encouraged to devote themselves to study. All this was set out in John Comyn's Foundation Charter of 1191 which was confirmed by a Bull of Pope Celestine III in the same year. The collegiate church was consecrated on St Patrick's Day 1192 and dedicated to 'God, Our Blessed Lady Mary and St Patrick', and about the same time Comyn's new palace was completed close to the church. This palace, known as St Sepulchre's, remained the seat of the archbishops of

Dublin until 1806 when it was sold to the Crown as a police barracks, which it still is today.

John Comyn died in 1212 and was succeeded by Henri de Loundres, generally known as Henry of London. He was a close friend of King John and, even after his enthronement as archbishop, still retained many lucrative appointments in England. Henry was present at the signing of Magna Carta in 1215 and his name may be seen among the signatories. Before King John died in 1216 he granted to Henry many additional estates and manors around Dublin in recompense, it is said, for his part in the building of Dublin Castle and the city walls at his own expense. King John is still perpetuated in St Patrick's as his head is carved in stone as the north terminal of the east arch of the choir, the head of Henry of London being represented as the south terminal.

Over both the dean's and precentor's stalls is a symbol of what appears to be a star and crescent (**6**). This had some association with King Richard I and was adopted by King John for the coinage minted in Ireland prior to his accession. The shape of the 'star and crescent' may, however, have altered with restorations over the centuries.

While Henry's policy was to continue Comyn's plans, he found the original charter to be incomplete so he issued further charters giving additional privileges to the canons and creating the offices of dean, precentor, chancellor and treasurer. These four officers or dignitaries were drawn from the chapter and were given extra churches to provide revenues suitable to their offices. Each was given a plot of land in the vicinity of the cathedral and they were instructed to build houses at their own expense. Henry also provided that all future deans should be elected by the chapter of canons from their own number, a privilege retained to this day. Having continued Comyn's adoption of the Sarum Constitution from England, Henry's work of remodelling the chapter of St Patrick's was now complete.

There are indications that before John

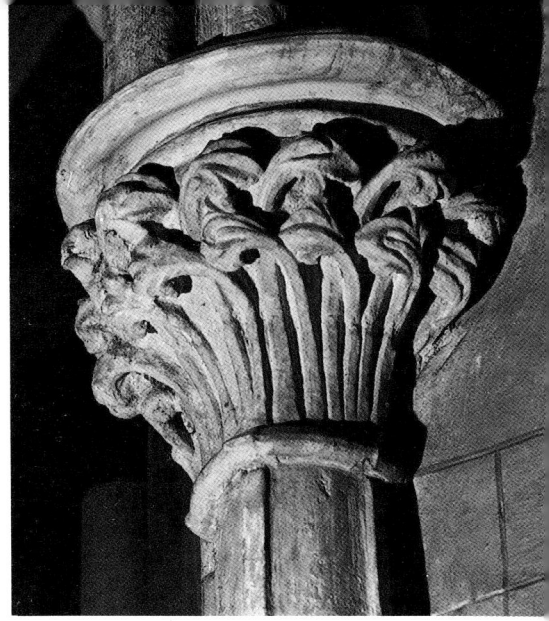

5   Thirteenth-century capital

Comyn died he had formed a project for a much greater building, more worthy of an archbishop, and undoubtedly Henry of London felt that this plan should be implemented. In the early 1220s he made preparations for the rebuilding of the cathedral on a more lofty scale and issued a special appeal in 1225. Thus began the construction of the present cathedral, in the Early English Gothic style, which continued for the next thirty years. Henry died in 1228 and his successor, Archbishop Luke, was responsible for the completion of the main building which was rededicated in 1254. Archbishop Fulk de Saundford, who followed Luke, in 1270 added the Lady Chapel (**7**), dedicated to the Blessed Virgin Mary. His tomb (**4**) may be seen in the north choir aisle.

A tower at the north-west end of the cathedral was part of the thirteenth-century building but this tower and part of the west nave were destroyed by fire in 1362. Through the energies of Archbishop Minot the damage was made good and the restoration was finished in 1370.

The date of the raising of the collegiate church to cathedral status is not known. While there is some acceptance of the fact that Henry of London may have been responsible soon after his appointment, there is evidence that the church became a cathedral during the episcopacy of John

Comyn. Henry was elected archbishop in 1212 by the chapters of both Christ Church and St Patrick's and the validity of this election was recognised by Pope Innocent III. It is therefore probable that St Patrick's had been raised to cathedral status before this date. From what we know of John Comyn's plans for the organisation and development, it seems that his intention was that St Patrick's should replace Christ Church, because having two cathedrals in one city, albeit one regular and one secular, would have been without precedent. The strong resistance of Christ Church to this scheme was, however, to be expected and its refusal to be deprived of its ancient privilege would have created the strange anomaly of two cathedrals each possessing the rights of the cathedral of the diocese. Comyn must have accepted this opposition but it must be remembered that while he was basically opposed to the monastic and regular character of Christ Church, he did give much assistance to the extensive Norman rebuilding which had been in progress there for many years.

In 1872, as a result of the disestablishment of the Church of Ireland, St Patrick's became the national cathedral, having a common relation with every diocese in Ireland, north and south, with canonical representation in the chapter from each diocese. Christ Church became the cathedral for the united dioceses of Dublin, Glendalough and Kildare and the metropolitan cathedral of the southern province of the Church. The diocese of Kildare was ceded to Meath in 1976.

The cathedral suffered much over the centuries due to desecration, fire, neglect and wear, and numerous efforts were made to carry out repairs and restorations although these were sadly limited by the money available. While Dean Pakenham carried out an excellent restoration of the Lady Chapel (**7**) in the 1850s, the main building was in a state of decay. But for the remarkable generosity of Sir Benjamin Guinness, who completely restored the fabric between 1860 and 1864 at a cost of about £160,000, the cathedral might not be standing today.

In the 1880s Sir Benjamin's third son, Sir Edward Guinness, later to become the first Earl of Iveagh, gave money for much needed improvements to the outside drainage and further continued the restoration of the interior. While the cathedral was in good condition at the beginning of this century, it was realised in recent decades that extensive renovation was again necessary, so following a public appeal in 1972 work commenced on major repairs and replacements to the whole fabric, including lighting, heating and general modernisation. Constant maintenance continues despite the heavy burden on the cathedral finances, but it is imperative that this ancient building is preserved at all costs. Inevitably through the years the fabric has undergone transformation, but a few of the original capitals (**5**) may be seen and most of the vaulting in the north and south choir aisles dates back to the thirteenth century.

The dean, precentor, chancellor and treasurer, the 'pillars of the choir' according to the old Sarum tradition, have their stalls at the four corners of the choir, the dean's 'Stall of Honour' at the south-west. The chapter of the cathedral now consists of the four dignitaries and twenty-two canons or prebendaries, each of whom is obliged to conduct services and preach for two weeks in the year. As in former days, a stall in the choir is allotted to each prebendary and the illustration shown (**16**) is the stall of the prebendary of St Audoen. These stalls were also used by the Knights of St Patrick. A member of a secular chapter formerly acted in two capacities and had two corresponding

6 Star and crescent symbol

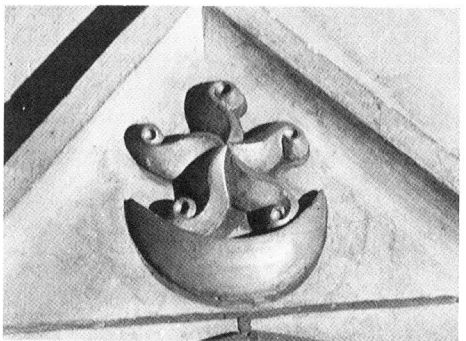

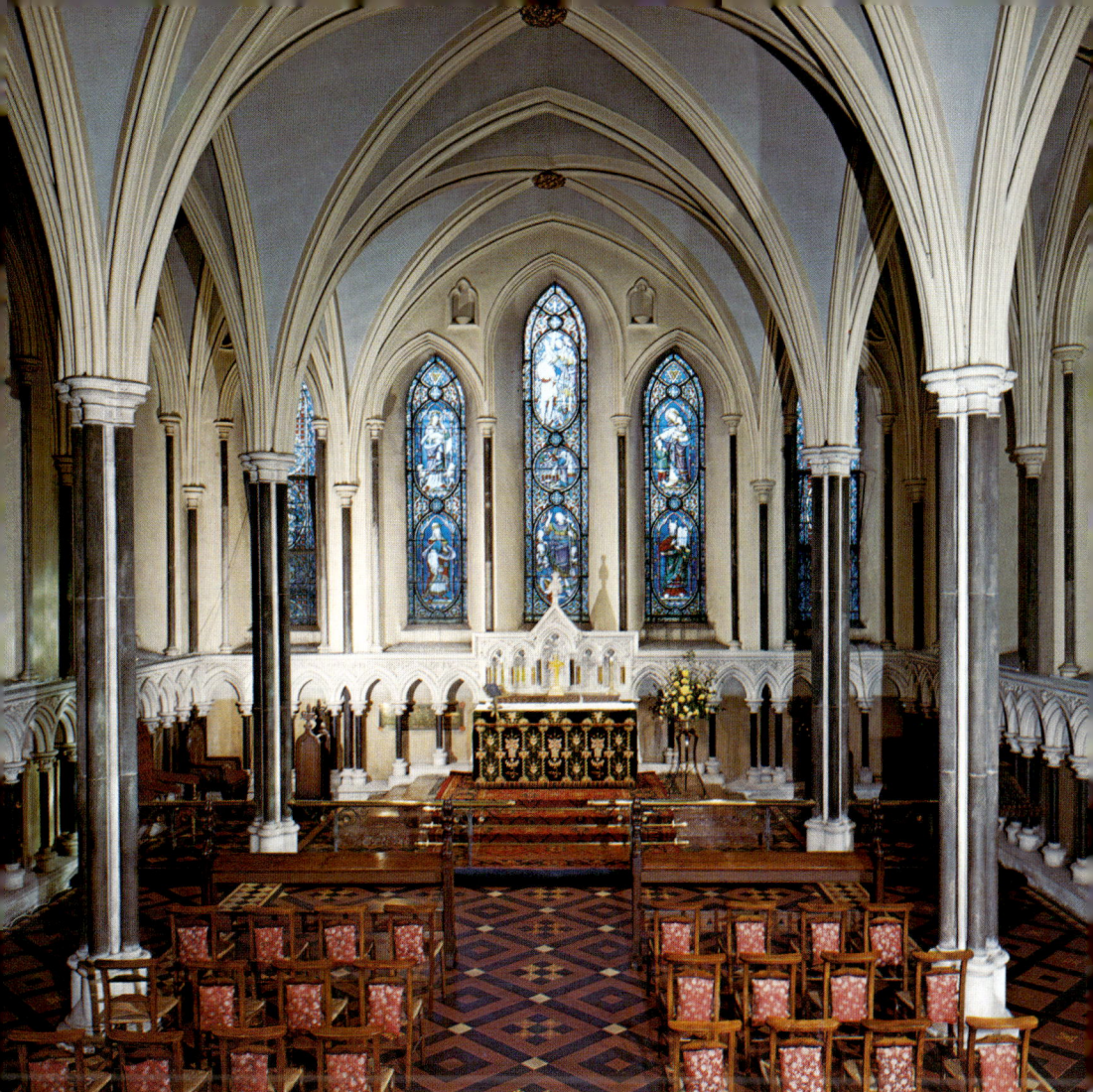

7 The Lady Chapel

sources of income. As a member of the chapter he was a canon and was entitled to a share in the common fund, but he was also a rector of a parish from which he derived, probably, the larger portion of his income, known as his 'prebend'. After the disestablishment, however, the connection of the canons with their prebendal parishes was severed, so the present canons are merely titular prebendaries.

The foundation of the College of Vicars Choral dates back to the time of Henry of London, and over the years various grants and privileges were given to them. They lived in the precincts, had a common hall, were obliged to attend regularly at services and to deputise for the prebendary to whom each was attached, during his absence. Following the disestablishment all these privileges disappeared, along with their properties, but the College of Vicars is still retained in name. Today there are four clerical vicars, representing the four dignitaries, six minor canons and seven lay vicars-choral. The minor canons were established in 1432 by Archbishop Talbot who also founded the Choir School in the same year.

One of the largest churches in Ireland, the cathedral is 91 metres long externally and the height of the nave vault (**24**) is 17 metres. Four bosses (**25**) can be seen along the centre of the choir vaulting, each representing one of the Evangelists – the angel, St Matthew, the winged lion, St Mark, the winged ox, St Luke and the eagle, St John. The quintuplet of windows

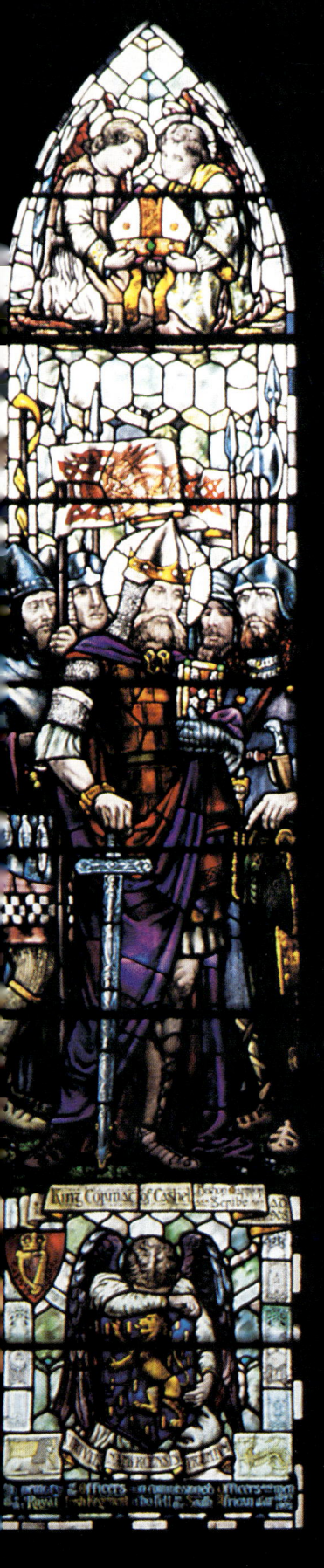

over the east arch (**20**) was erected by Lord Iveagh in 1901; it represents St Columba, St Patrick and St Brigid with allegorical figures at each side and is the work of Clayton & Bell.

The Reformation period was a time of much significance for St Patrick's. In 1537 Thomas Cromwell issued an order that all images of saints in the choir were to be demolished. A few years later all the cathedral's revenues, estates and possessions were surrendered to King Henry VIII and his commissioners, and the dean at the time, Edward Bassenet, who was a staunch supporter of the king, actually imprisoned the members of the chapter until they assented. Dean Bassenet also surrendered the deanery, but not without a handsome reward which consisted of a good pension and the leases of a number of properties. The other dignitaries and canons also received pensions.

Continuing his father's policies, King Edward VI reduced the cathedral to the status of a parish church and directed that part of the building should be used as a court-house. He also issued instructions to repaint the walls with passages or texts from the Scriptures. However, a charter of Philip and Mary in 1555 restored to St Patrick's its former rights and in the first year of the reign of Queen Elizabeth it was enacted that the English Liturgy must be used with the Book of Common Prayer of 1549. Much restoration to the fabric was necessary in 1555 because about eleven years earlier the great stone roof of the nave had collapsed at the west end and destroyed many ancient monuments. In 1560 the first public clock in Dublin was erected on the tower of the cathedral.

St Patrick's again suffered during the Commonwealth period about 100 years later. In 1647 the use of the Prayer Book was forbidden and in 1651 the building was turned to profane uses – courts-martial were held inside the church and Oliver Cromwell is said to have used part of the building as a stable for the horses of his troops. However, in 1660 the cathedral was again restored and at a great service in 1661 twelve bishops were consecrated.

8 The King Cormac window

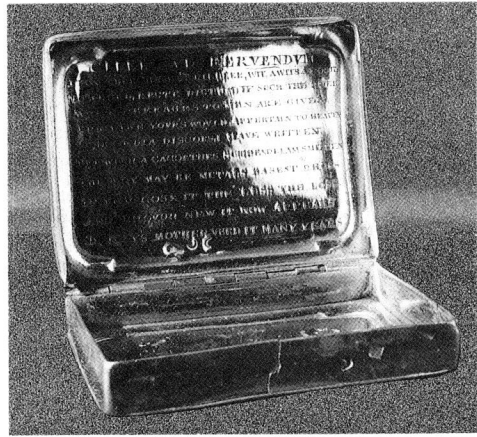
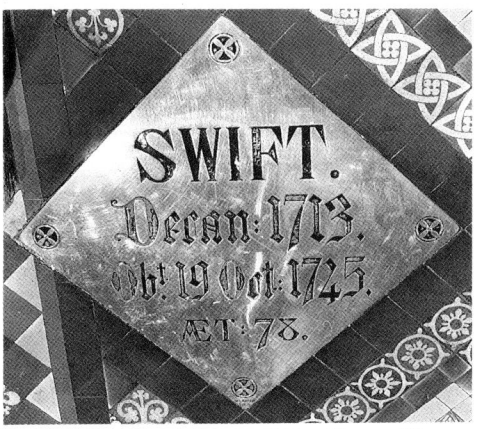
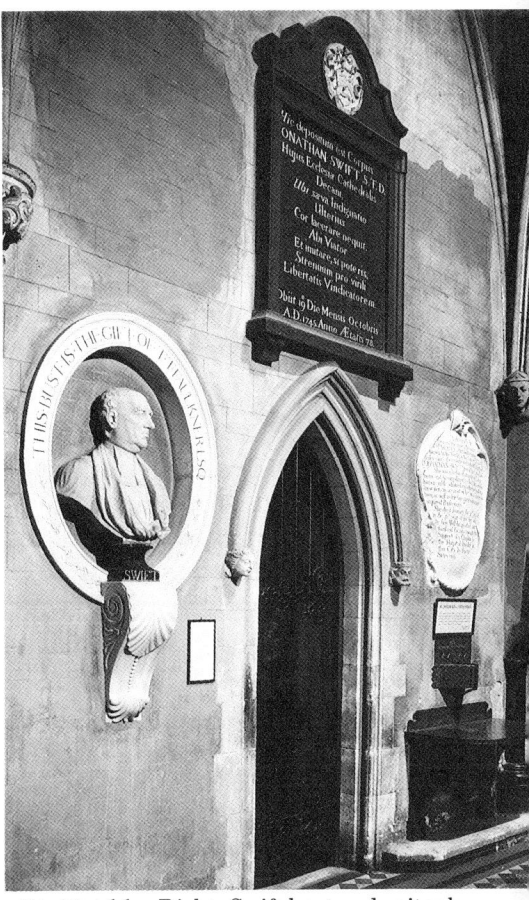

9 Top: Swift snuff-box **10** Above: The grave of Swift **11** Right: Swift bust and epitaph

The first university in Ireland was founded in St Patrick's Cathedral in 1320 due to the efforts of Archbishop de Bicknor, and the dean, William Rodyard, was appointed the first chancellor. This had the approval of Pope Clement V and the university continued in some form until the end of the fifteenth century when lack of funds caused it to close. In 1547 Archbishop Browne tried unsuccessfully to revive it, and in 1584 Queen Elizabeth issued instructions 'to consider how a college may be erected'. St Patrick's was considered unsuitable and the site of All Hallows' Priory was selected for the foundation of Trinity College in 1591.

The first provost of the new university was Adam Loftus, who also held the archbishopric of Dublin. Some years earlier he had been Dean of St Patrick's, and on his death in 1605 he was buried in the cathedral, although the vault has since disappeared. His successor was Archbishop Thomas Jones, whose monument (**23**) can still be seen at the west end of the north aisle. This monument, erected in 1628, commemorates the archbishop as a kneeling effigy in the upper portion, attired in his robes as Lord Chancellor of Ireland. The recumbent figure below, of a knight in armour, represents his son, Viscount Ranelagh. This memorial was restored in 1731 by a descendant, Lady Catherine Jones, at Dean Swift's request, but it has since suffered some damage.

The largest monument in the cathedral is that of the Boyle family at the southwest end of the nave. This massive structure (**15, 32**) was erected by the great Earl of Cork in 1632, during his lifetime, principally in memory of his second wife Katherine, and included in the numerous figures are the Earl, his wife, children, his wife's parents and her grandfather Robert Weston, a former dean. This monument was sited originally in front

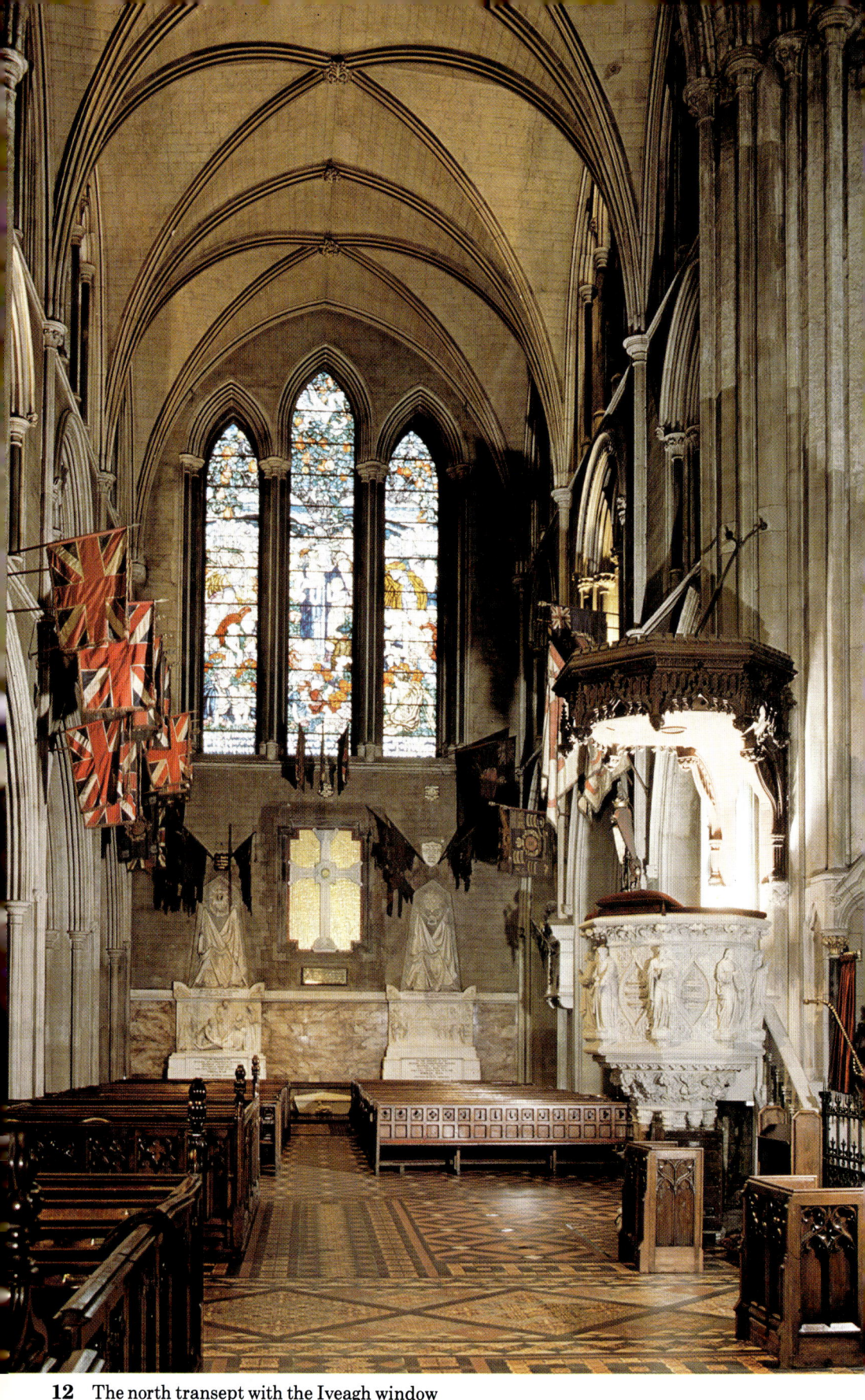

12 The north transept with the Iveagh window

of the east arch of the sanctuary, but immediately after its erection there were strong objections from Archbishop Laud and the Earl of Strafford which resulted in it being moved to the south side of the sanctuary. It was relocated to its present position during the Guinness restoration.

At the end of the nave (**24**), on the west wall, are paintings in oil representing the coats of arms of five archbishops of Dublin: Hugh Curwen, Thomas Jones, Launcelot Bulkeley, James Margetson and Michael Boyle. These men held the See of Dublin between 1555 and 1678 but the arms of Adam Loftus, archbishop from 1567 to 1605, are missing. These paintings, recently restored, have been in the cathedral for probably 300 years and are of particular interest as they are painted on wood panels.

Beside the Jones monument is an attractive bas-relief of Turlough Carolan (**21**), last of the Irish harpers, which was executed by J.V. Hogan about 1874. Lady Morgan, a well-known Dublin philanthropist in the early nineteenth century, left money in her will for this to be commissioned. Carolan was a contemporary of Swift and an occasional visitor to the deanery.

The Most Illustrious Order of St Patrick was founded for Irish peers in 1783 by King George III and the first Grand Master was Earl Temple, later Marquess of Buckingham, who was Lord Lieutenant at the time. His statue (**22**) can be seen in the north aisle and is the work of Edward Smyth, the noted Irish sculptor. The Marquess is attired in the elaborate robes and regalia of the Grand Master.

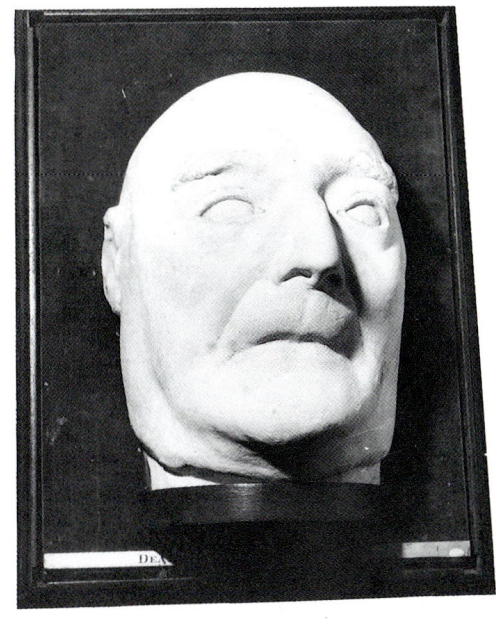

13   The death-mask of Swift

14   'Swift Corner'

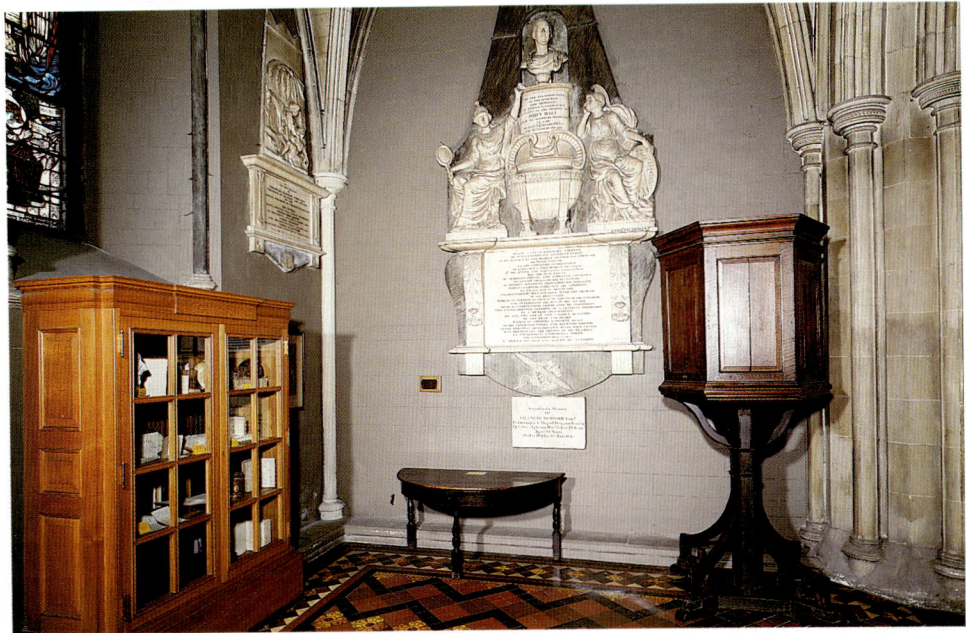

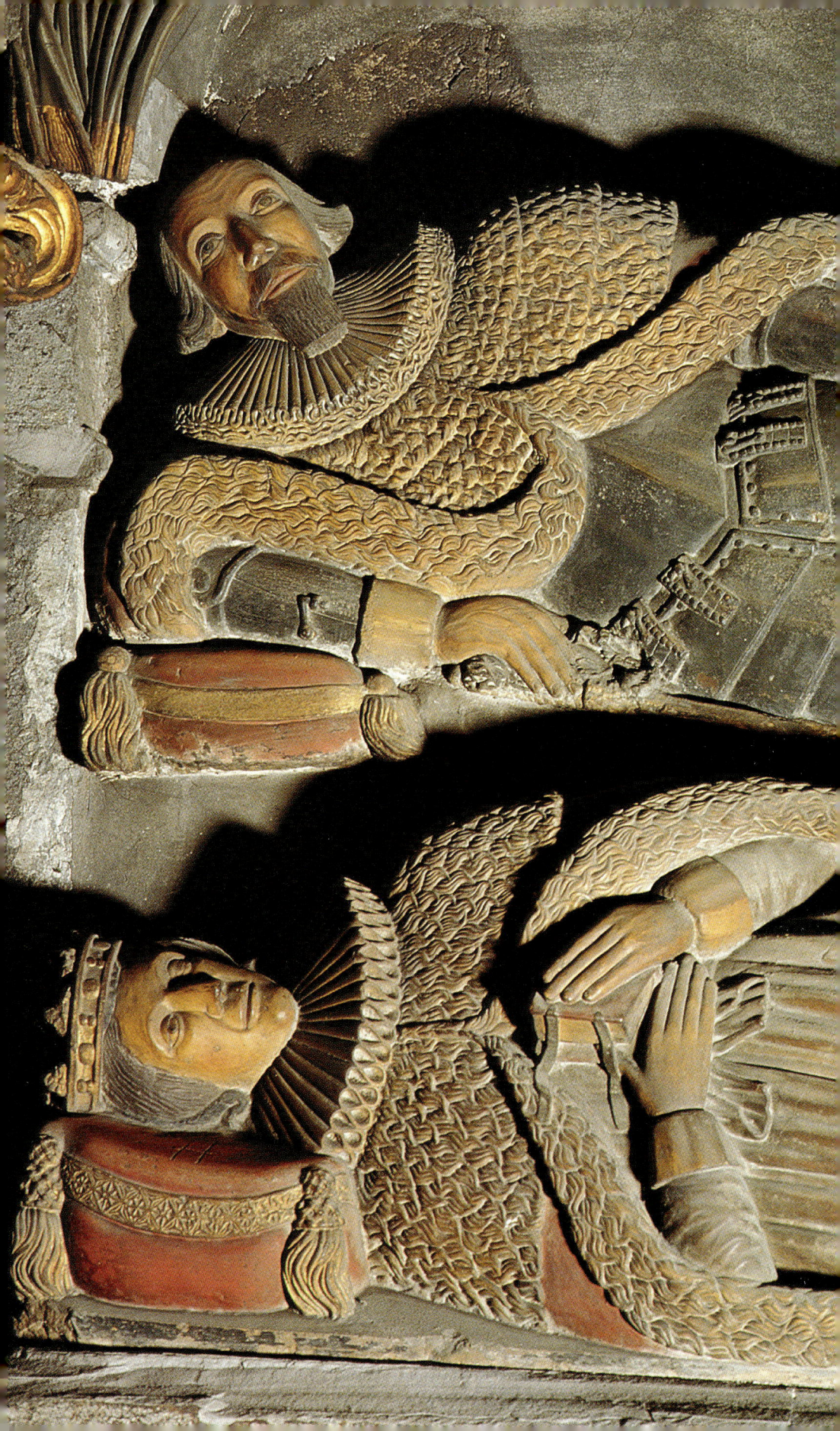

It was decided that St Patrick's Cathedral should be the chapel of the Order and Dean Cradock was appointed registrar. Each knight was instructed to send his banner, a symbolic sword, helmet and crest to the cathedral to be placed over his stall and to have an escutcheon made of his arms on a brass plate and affixed to the back of the stall. The illustration (**16**) shows the arms of the Earl of Roden and below, those of the Earl of Granard. In 1871 the connection of the Order with St Patrick's ceased but the banners and insignia of the knights at that time still remain, lending an element of colour to the choir (**3**). The standard over the dean's stall, on the south side of the choir, is that of Queen Victoria, the titular head of the Order, but as a woman she was not allowed to bear a crest or sword. Above the precentor's stall, opposite, is the standard of Prince Arthur, Duke of Connaught, the Queen's third son. He bore the royal arms with a label of three points, on the centre point a cross of St George and on each of the other points a fleur-de-lis. Few ceremonies were held in the cathedral, however, and generally it was used on the occasions of royal visits. St Patrick's Hall in Dublin Castle was the normal place for investitures and meetings and there similar banners may be seen. The last great ceremony held in St Patrick's was in 1868 when the Prince of Wales was invested as a knight.

Affixed to the wall in the south choir aisle are four old brasses. That nearest the Lady Chapel is in memory of Sir Henry Wallop, Vice-Treasurer of Ireland, who died in 1599. Next is a memorial to Robert Sutton, dean of the cathedral from 1527 to 1528. The short time that Sutton was dean he spent outside the country because of ill-health and to avoid the plague which was then prevalent, never once setting foot inside his cathedral. After Sutton's death, Thomas Darcy was elected dean but died after only ten months in office. He was succeeded by Geoffry Fyche to whom the next brass was erected; it is somewhat similar in design to that of Robert Sutton. The translation of the inscription reads, 'Pray

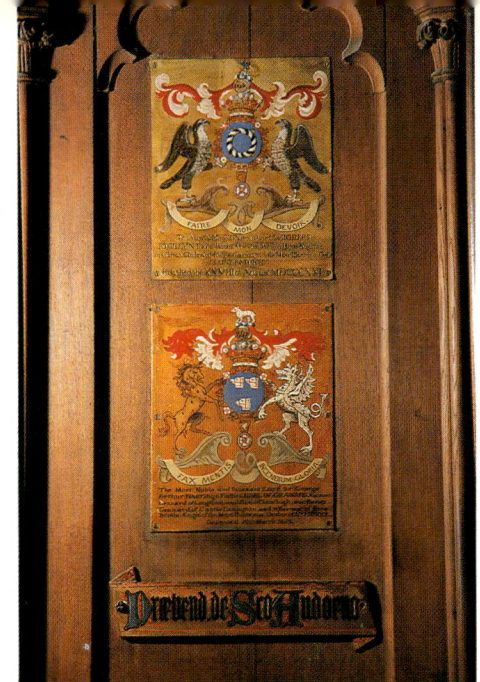

16 Hatchments on a choir-stall

for the soul of Master Geoffry Fyche, Dean of this Cathedral Church who closed his mortal course on 8th April in the year of Our Lord 1537 and was buried in this tomb. May God be merciful to his soul. Amen.' The cape or amice worn by Dean Fyche in this superb brass is inlaid with silver. The fourth brass is in memory of Sir Edward Ffiton, who was sent to Ireland by Queen Elizabeth as Lord President of the Council in Connaught and Thomond. He died in 1579 and on the brass he is represented with his wife and their fifteen children.

There are many memorial brasses in the cathedral but all the others are of a much later date. On the floor in the choir is the well-restored brass of Richard Talbot, Archbishop of Dublin from 1417 to 1449. The slab in which the brass is set is the original matrix, discovered in the churchyard in 1902. The reproduction of the brass was carried out by Barkentin & Krall in 1919 through the generosity of Lord Iveagh.

The pulpit (**30**) was the gift of Sir Benjamin Guinness as a tribute to Dean Pakenham who died in 1863 just as Sir Benjamin's restoration was being finished. It was designed and executed by Henry Lane of Dublin and is made from

15 Detail from the Boyle monument

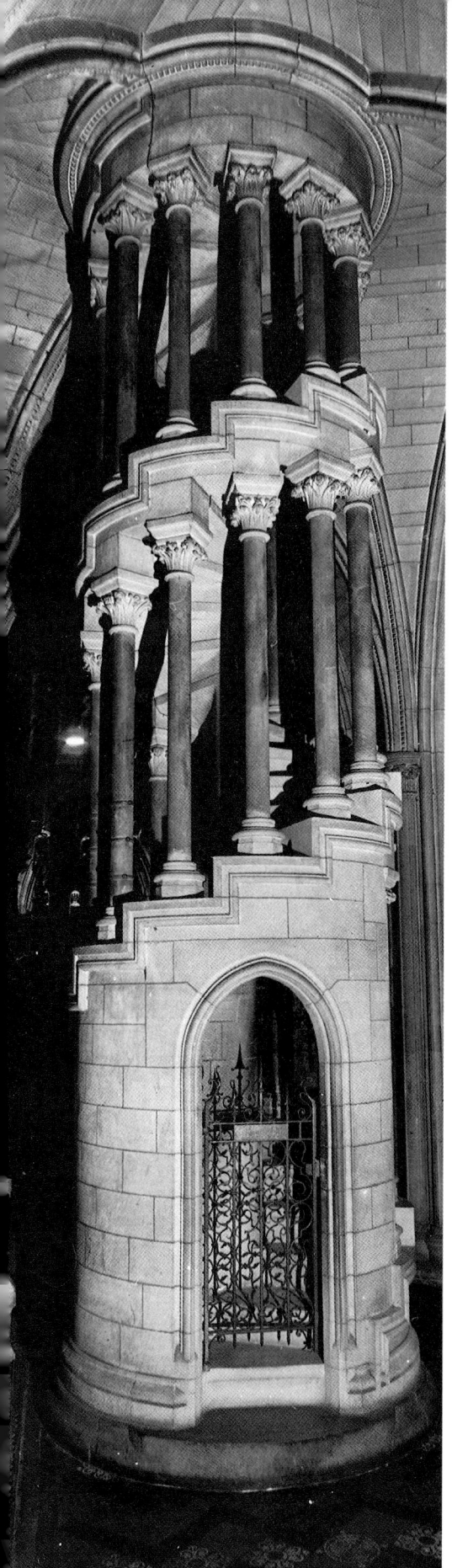

Caen stone and Irish coloured marbles. The sounding-board was presented shortly afterwards by Mr John Robinson who also gave all the chairs in the nave. The fine brass lectern, in the shape of an eagle, was presented in memory of Dean Jellett who died in 1902.

The north transept of the cathedral (**12**) was used as the parish church of St Nicholas Without (the city) from the middle of the fourteenth century to the early part of the nineteenth century. In the Guinness restoration it once more became part of the main cathedral. It contains a number of war memorials and from the walls hang many of the colours of old Irish regiments, now disbanded. The window of three lights (**12**) was erected in 1935 by the children of the first Earl of Iveagh, in his memory, and was designed by Sir Frank Brangwyn.

Jonathan Swift was appointed dean in 1713 and his name is indissolubly connected with the history of St Patrick's and indeed of Dublin. A man of remarkable character, he attended to the interests of the cathedral with much ability and industry. His numerous works and tracts created for him a place among the great writers in the English tongue and he is remembered in St Patrick's in many ways. Desirous to keep alive the memory of the cathedral's connection with the past, he devoted much time and thought to the maintenance of its traditions and the preservation of its monuments. A number of relics can be seen in the 'Swift Corner' (**14**) of the north transept. A bookcase contains a death-mask (**13**), some of his publications and books written later on his life and works. Nearby is an altar-table from his church at Laracor and a movable pulpit from which he preached in the cathedral.

Swift died in 1745 after a long illness and was buried in the south-west of the nave at midnight, near Stella, his great friend, in accordance with his own wishes. A simple brass plate marks his grave (**10**). A few yards away on the south wall is a bust (**11**) presented by

17 Staircase to the organ-loft

the nephew of his principal publisher, Thomas Faulkner, on the right is a memorial to Stella – not written by Swift – and over the doorway is his famous epitaph, written by himself. In translation it reads, 'Here is laid the body of Jonathan Swift, Doctor of Divinity, Dean of this Cathedral Church, where fierce indignation can no longer rend the heart. Go, traveller, and imitate if you can, this earnest and dedicated champion of liberty. He died on the 19th day of October, 1745 AD. Aged 78 years.'

Kept with the cathedral plate is a snuff-box (**9**) once the property of Dean Swift. Inside the lid is a strange inscription in a mixture of Latin and English, interspersed with obscure puns, typical of Swift's style. The heading reads 'Celer ad Fervendum', which possibly means 'Swift to Boyle'. The inscription suggests that Swift presented it to John Boyle, Earl of Orrery.

It is a tragedy that no stained-glass windows from earlier than the nineteenth century have survived, but there are some excellent examples of Irish, English and Scottish craftsmanship of the Victorian and Edwardian periods, particularly in the smaller windows. The illustration shown (**8**) is a memorial to the men of the Royal Irish Regiment who fell in the South African War. It was designed by

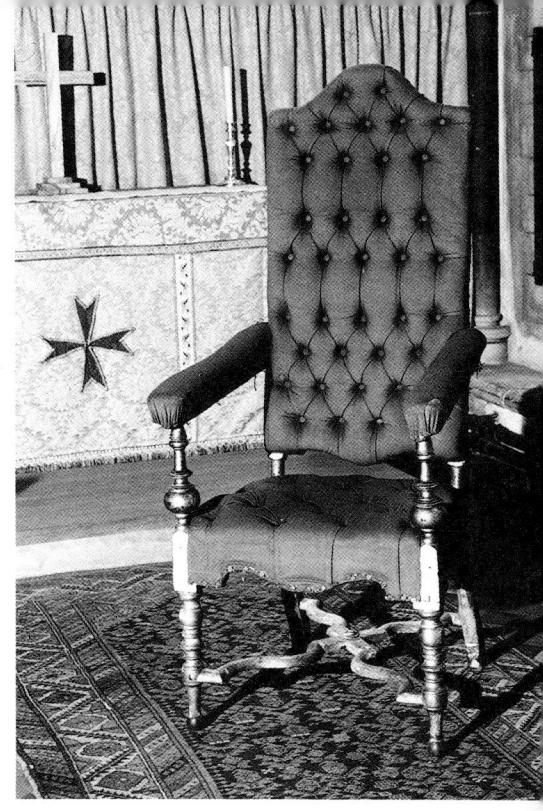

18 The King William chair

Sara Purser, painted by A.E. Child and executed by An Tur Gloine in Dublin. The motif is King Cormac of Cashel.

The floor of the cathedral is set in encaustic tiles which were laid in 1882. The designs were based on some medieval tiles discovered under the floor of a part of the south transept.

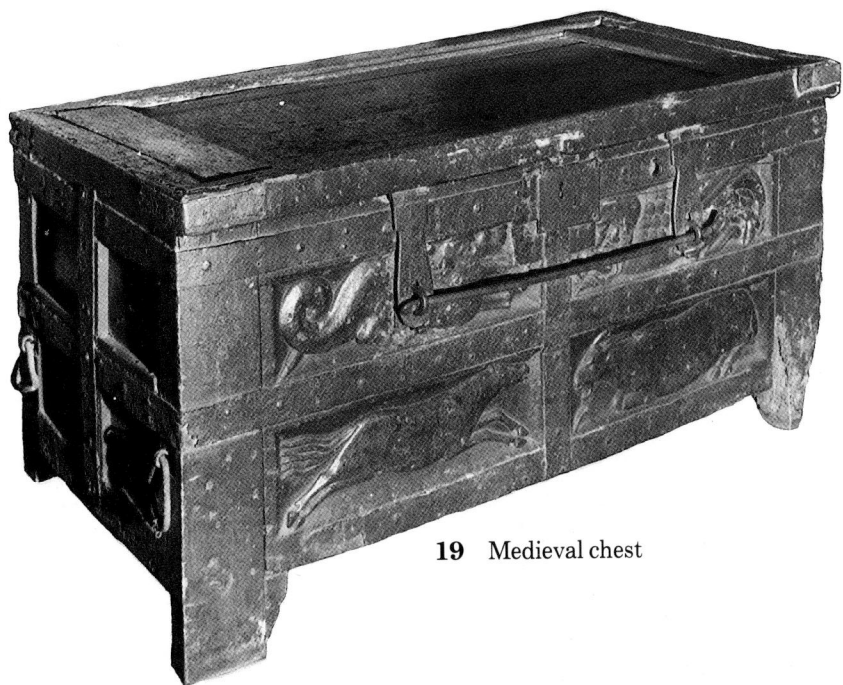

19 Medieval chest

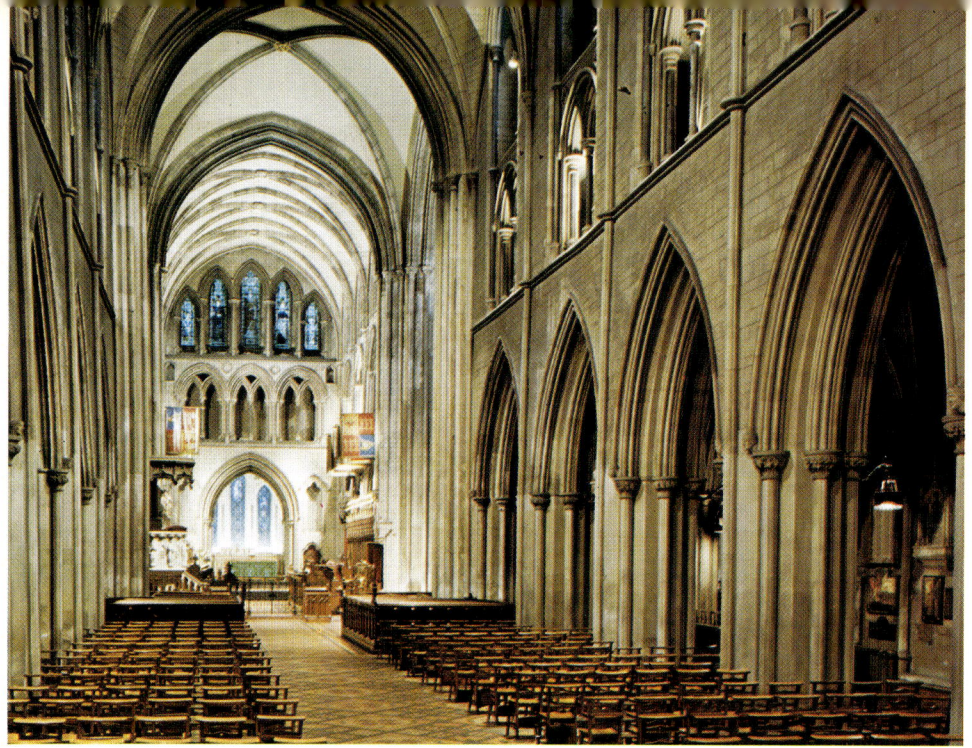

20 The nave, facing east

In former days the central part of the south transept was used as a chapter-house and the old door (**26**), with a hole cut in it, is still preserved, now placed at the west end of the nave. It is known as 'The Door of Reconciliation'. The Earl of Ormonde and the Earl of Kildare nearly came to blows inside the church on an eventful day in 1492. Ormonde and his followers, being pursued by the Kildare contingent, sought refuge in the chapter-house, but a truce was soon agreed and a hole was cut in the door so that they could shake hands. Lord Ormonde was still suspicious, but the first move was made by Lord Kildare who extended his hand which was duly grasped. Thus the quarrel ended, although it proved to be only temporary.

The eastern part of the transept was originally the Chapel of St Paul and it was here that the ancient tiles were found. During most of the eighteenth and the early part of the nineteenth century the fabric of the cathedral deteriorated considerably, and probably during this period St Paul's Chapel fell into disuse, but the chapels of St Peter and St Stephen remain at the east ends of the north and south choir aisles. Both have been restored in recent years.

In the middle of the seventeenth century large numbers of French Protestant refugees came to Ireland and many settled in Dublin. As they had no place of worship the Dean and Chapter allowed them to use the Lady Chapel (**7**) subject to certain conditions. Alterations were carried out to make the chapel self-contained and in 1666 an opening service was held, attended by the Lord Lieutenant. The Huguenots used this chapel until the late eighteenth century, by which time they had gradually merged with the Irish population.

In the 1780s John Wesley ministered in St Patrick's on a number of occasions during his evangelistic campaigns in Ireland.

Before the Guinness restoration the shape of the interior of the cathedral was somewhat different from what it is today. A rood screen at the west of the crossing divided the nave and choir and above the screen was the organ. For a long period there were three churches in the same building: St Nicholas' in the north transept, the Huguenots in the Lady

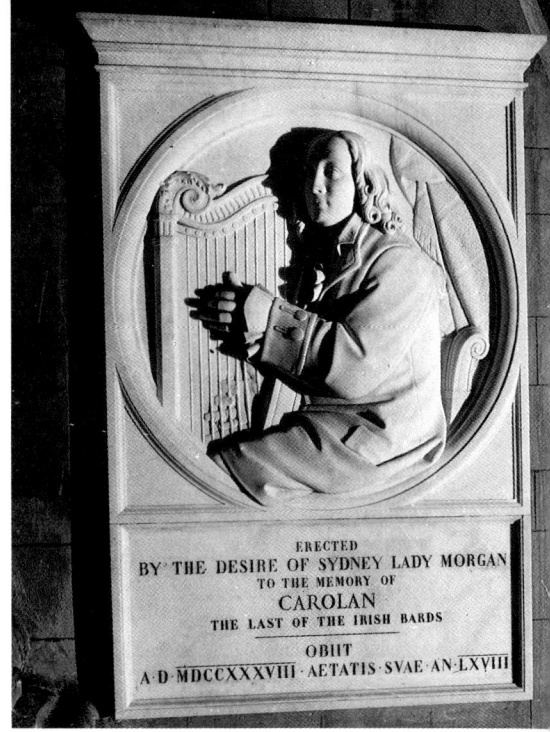

21 The Carolan memorial

Chapel and the cathedral itself. Apart from the importance of the restoration work by Sir Benjamin, the opening of the whole ground area was additionally significant as it unified the fine architectural details of the building and provided more space for worshippers.

The cathedral is rich in monuments, but although there are records of numerous interments in medieval times, few of the monuments from this period remain due to the effects of storms, floods and destruction during the troublesome periods of the sixteenth and seventeenth centuries. There are some good examples of eighteenth-century monumental sculpture, particularly in the south transept, and perhaps the finest is that erected in memory of Lady Doneraile who died in 1761 (**28**). It is the work of Simon Vierpyl.

Other important monuments in the transept are those commemorating three archbishops: Marsh, who founded the library beside the cathedral, Smyth and Whately. Perhaps the most humble of all is a plaque erected by Swift in memory of his servant, Alexander McGee. Nearby, set on a corbel, is a strange statue (**27**) which is reputed to be of St Patrick and, although there are references to it as St Patrick over the centuries, it is more probable that it is an effigy of a cleric, perhaps of the fourteenth century. The head is incongruous and was added at a later date. In the south aisle are memorials to two Presidents of Ireland: Dr Douglas Hyde, first President, 1938 to 1945, and Erskine Childers, who was elected fourth President in 1974, but died suddenly in the same year.

The cathedral has an interesting collection of silver plate although much of it was acquired during the last 200 years. In 1779 all the plate was stolen and the chapter ordered a new set of nine pieces from Richard Williams of Dublin. This is of superb quality and it is recorded that its total cost was £112.

In 1471 Archbishop Tregury presented 'a pair of organs' for use in the Lady

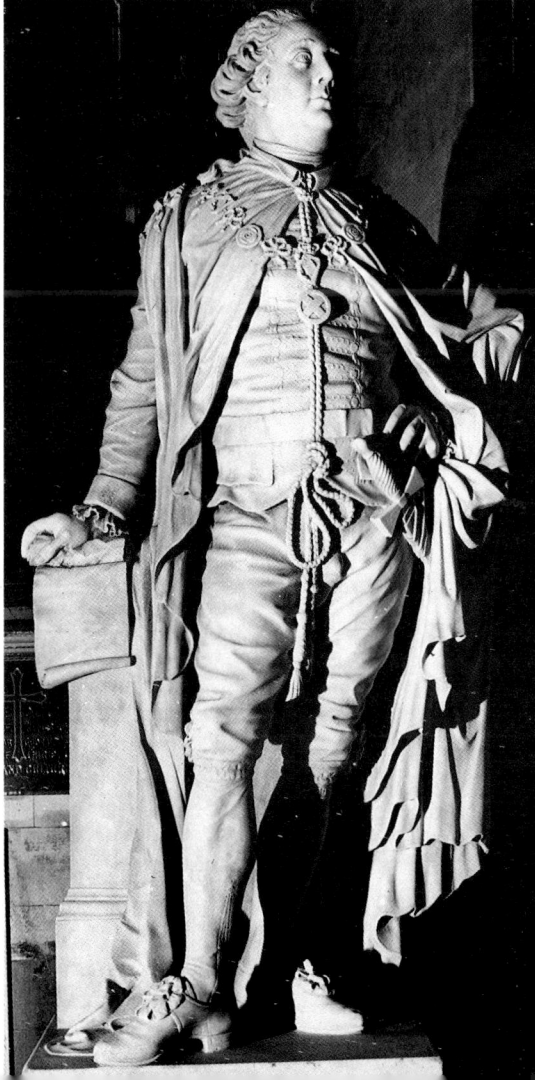

22 The Buckingham statue

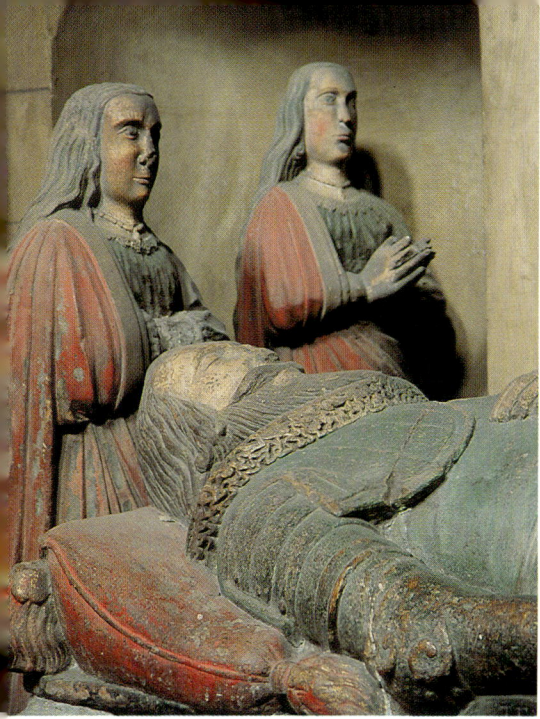

23 Detail of the Jones monument

Chapel, but the first important instrument was that of Renatus Harris in 1695. Rebuilt and improved many times, it lasted for 200 years. The present superb instrument, by H. Willis, was built in 1902, the gift of the first Lord Iveagh, and is the largest church organ in Ireland. It was rebuilt by J.W.Walker in 1964, 30 years later a further large scale restoration was carried out by Harrison and Harrison of Durham returning to the original character of the instrument as created by Willis. Access to the organ is by means of a handsome spiral staircase (**17**), designed by Sir Thomas Drew, which is in the north transept.

The choir has achieved much fame and the high standard of music, developed over the last 100 years by Dr Charles Marchant, Dr George Hewson, William Greig and John Dexter, is nobly maintained. Many important services have been held in the cathedral over the years, some with great ceremony, but perhaps the climax of the year is the traditional service on Christmas Eve of Nine Lessons and Carols, which culminates in an impressive rendering of 'Hark, the Herald Angels Sing' to the music of Handel's *Judas Maccabeus.*

24 The choir and nave, facing west

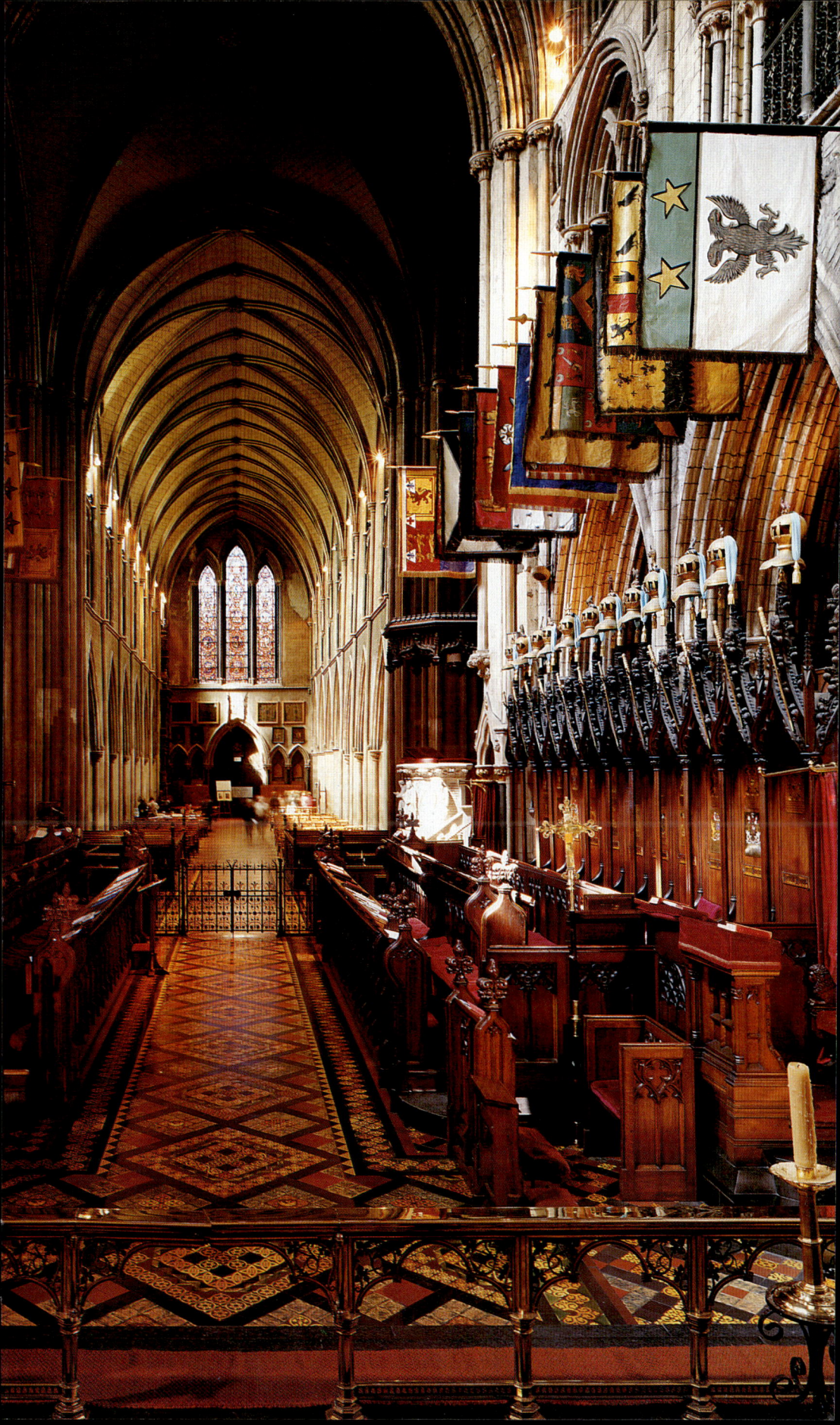

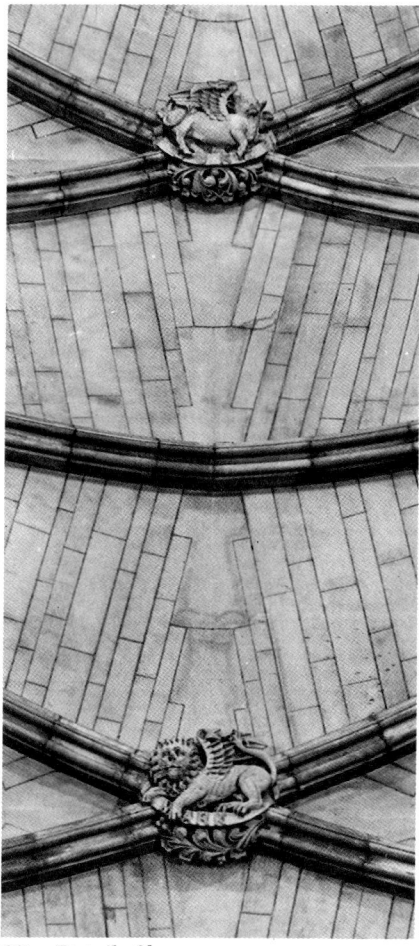

25 Detail of bosses

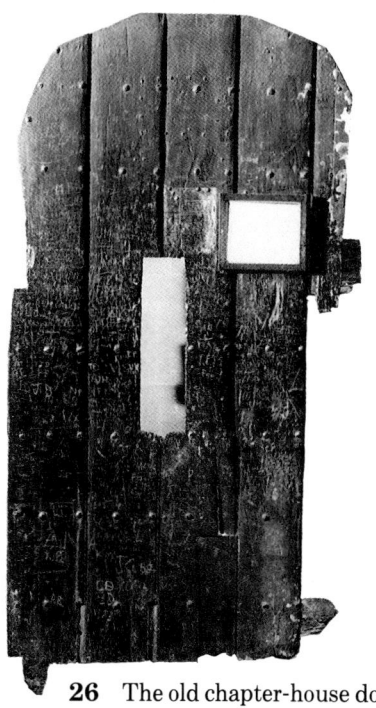

26 The old chapter-house door

27 Figure of 'St Patrick'

In the Minot tower the uppermost chamber is the belfry. The bells are rung on Sundays and on other special occasions by the St Patrick's Cathedral Amateur Society of Change Ringers, continuing a tradition extending over 700 years. Above the tower is a spire erected in 1749, after a design by George Semple. The cost was defrayed by a legacy left for that purpose by Bishop Stearne, a former dean. The tower is 43 metres high and 12 metres square at the base, with walls 3 metres thick. Although it was generally in a sound condition, an extensive cleaning

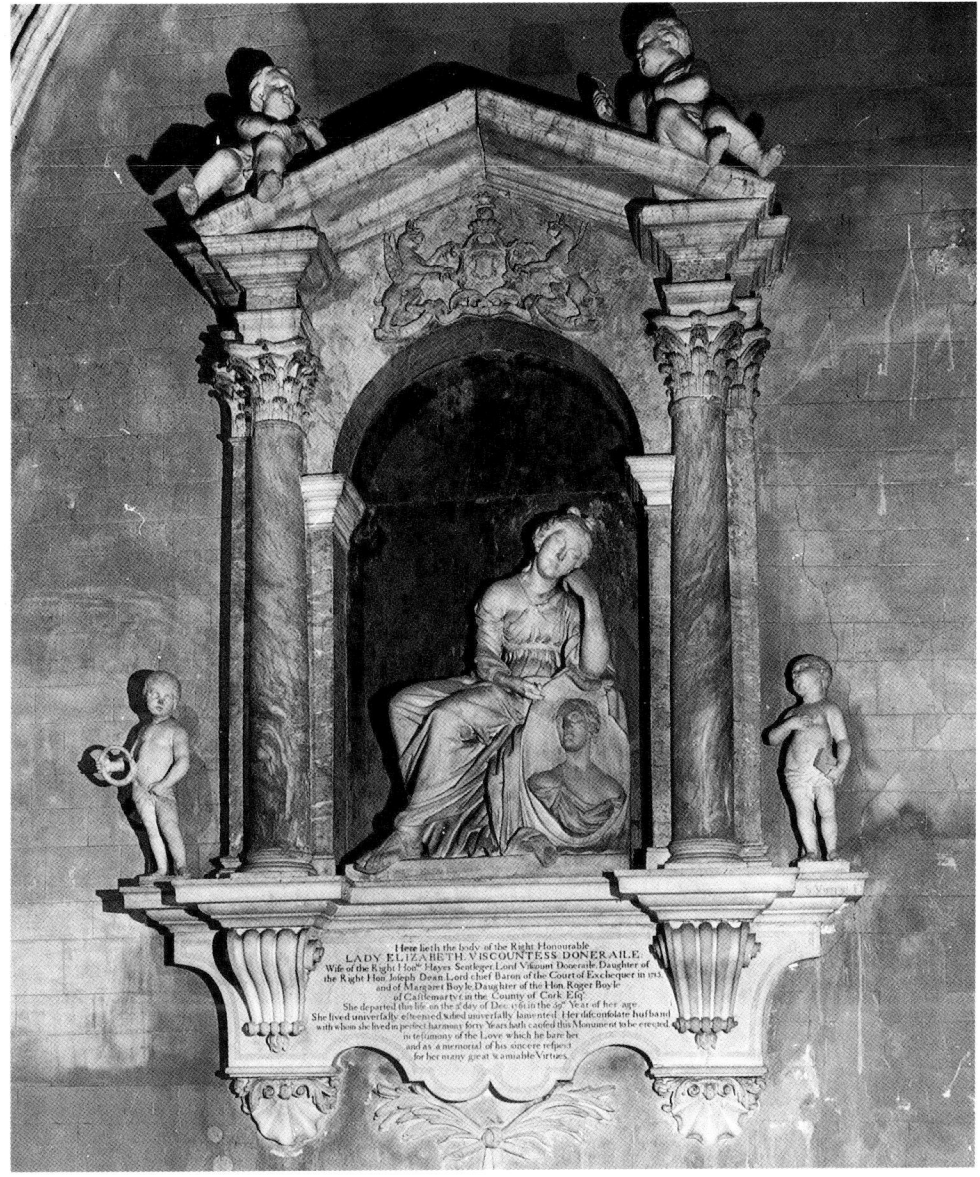

28 The Doneraile monument

and repointing operation was carried out in 1974 to preserve it. The spire is 31 metres high.

An old medieval chest (**19**), which bears some curious carvings of animals, may be seen in the north transept near the organ staircase. No doubt it was used for vestments, church plate and other valuable items. Altar frontals are now kept in another chest, behind the main altar, which was made in 1897 from the old oak which was used for the construction of the beams in the Minot tower. An old high-backed chair (**18**) in the Lady Chapel is said to have been used by King William III when he attended a service in the cathedral after the Battle of the Boyne.

At the south-west end of the cathedral is the baptistery (**31**), the oldest part of the building and a reminder of the early foundation of John Comyn. The vaulting is of earlier date than the main building and it is probable that this was the entrance to Comyn's church. Nothing is known of the history of the medieval stone font, still in use after many generations. The floor tiles are those which were

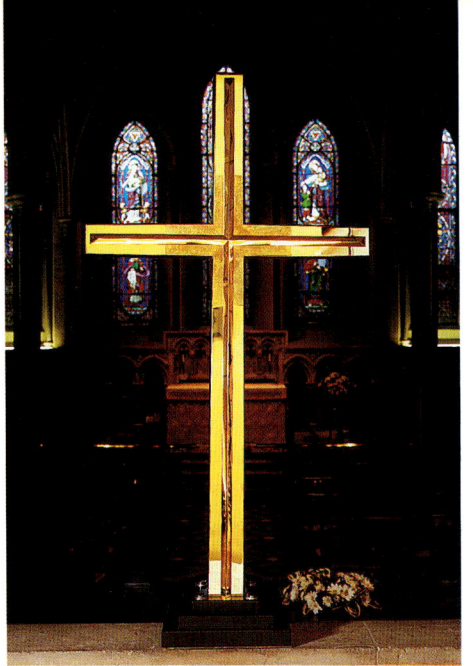

29 This fine altar cross, which is 132 cm in height, was given to the cathedral in 1995 in memory of Cecil Harmsworth King. It was designed and made by the well-known goldsmith and silversmith, Gerald Benney.

policy on his house for £1,300. After the fire he was thanked by the chapter for his foresight. In the hall and on the staircase is some good plasterwork typical of the period, and in the dining-room hang portraits of most of the deans in the last 250 years. Dominating the whole room, however, is Francis Bindon's famous painting of Swift. On the staircase is a magnificent full-length portrait of the Marquess of Buckingham, by Robert Hunter.

Also in the Close is the Choir School founded in 1432 for the education of the choristers. The Grammar School was established later in 1547. Both schools were rebuilt in the 1980s.

reset after their removal from the south transept. The baptistery cross was the work of the well-known Irish sculptor Oisin Kelly (1915-81).

To the east and south of the cathedral is a graveyard of great antiquity. Even at the time when Comyn built his church and palace, much of it had long been in disuse. Many famous Irishmen and many who had close connections with St Patrick's lie buried here. Although Sir Benjamin Guinness is interred elsewhere, he is commemorated on the south lawn by a fine statue by John Foley, a sculptor whose work can be seen in many public places in Dublin.

Nearby, to the south, is the Deanery House. Apart from references to those who resided in it, practically nothing is known of the building prior to about 1710 when John Stearne was dean. It seems that he considered the deanery too small and proceeded to rebuild it, very likely to accommodate his extensive library. In April 1781 a serious fire destroyed the north side of the house but this was rebuilt in 1781-2. Dean Cradock occupied the deanery at this time and it is recorded that in 1780 he took out an insurance

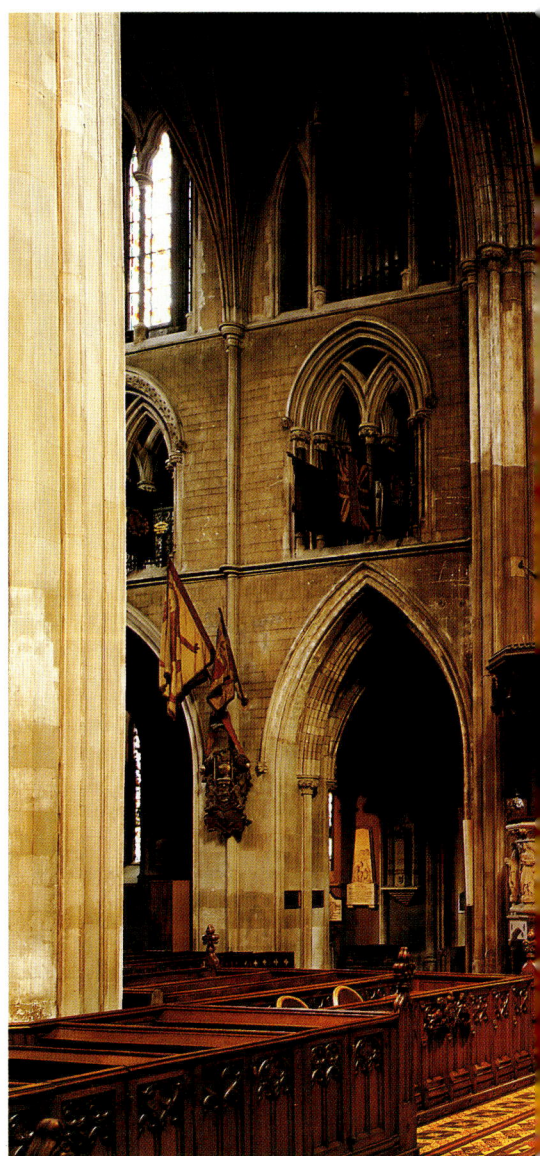

30 The choir and part of the north transept

In olden days all the dignitaries, together with the vicars and minor canons, held properties in the vicinity, and the precincts of the cathedral were considerably larger than they are today. St Patrick's Close, the street which runs by the south of the cathedral, was constructed by Sir Benjamin Guinness when he had completed his restoration. The eastern part of the street had been part of the deanery garden.

Nowadays all ancient buildings present a problem to those who are responsible for them and St Patrick's is no exception. Old endowments have dwindled and its future depends largely on the generosity of those who regard it as part of the heritage of Ireland. As one of the major tourist attractions in Dublin as well as the national cathedral, it is visited annually by many thousands of people, many from far-off countries. Members of all Christian denominations are welcome to attend the services. Visitors cannot fail to be impressed by the history, the spiritual atmosphere and the great music which continue a tradition of worship on this site for over fifteen hundred years. St Patrick's is a lasting memorial to the great churchmen, craftsmen and benefactors who have made such notable contributions to bring it to its present glory.

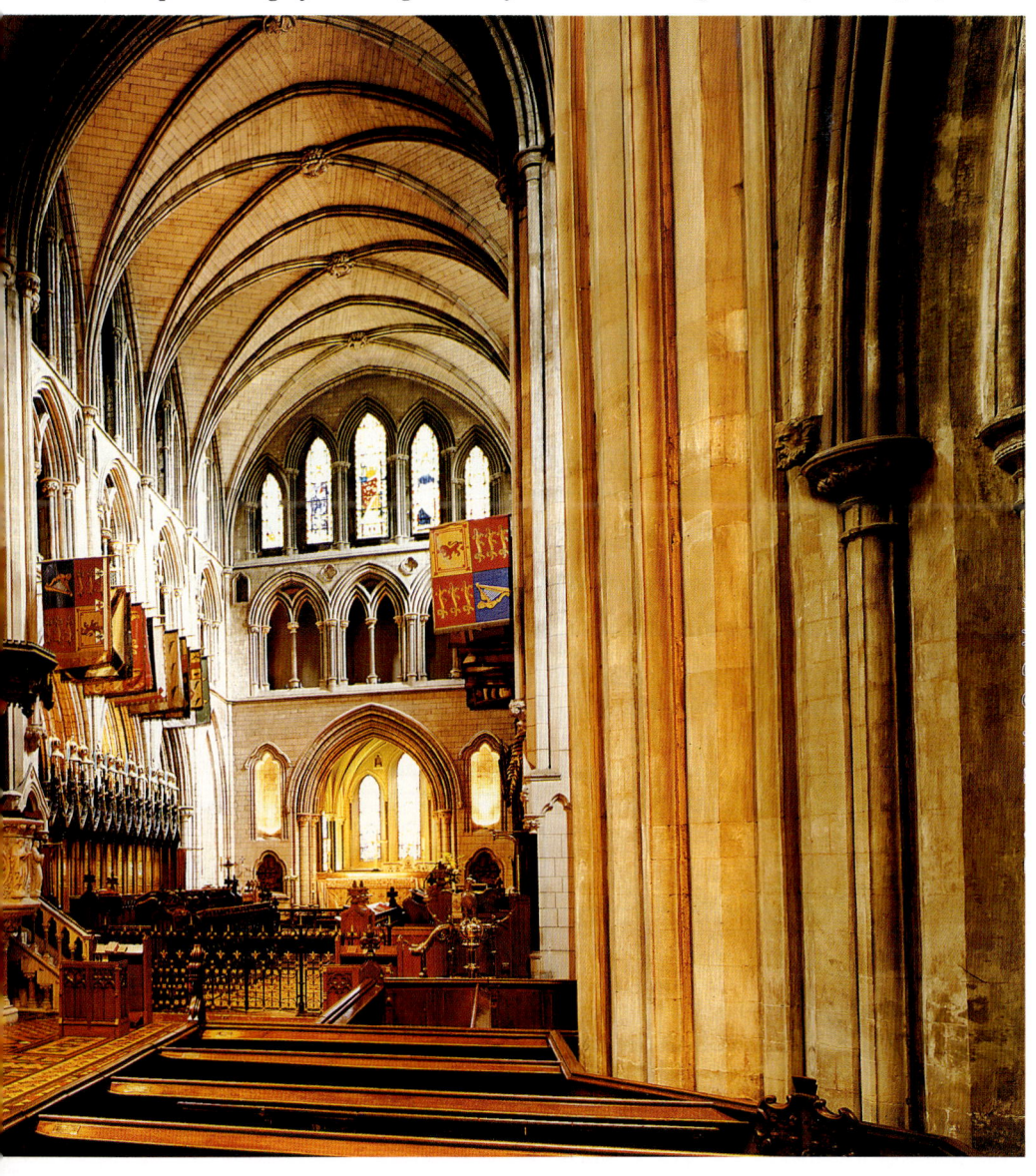

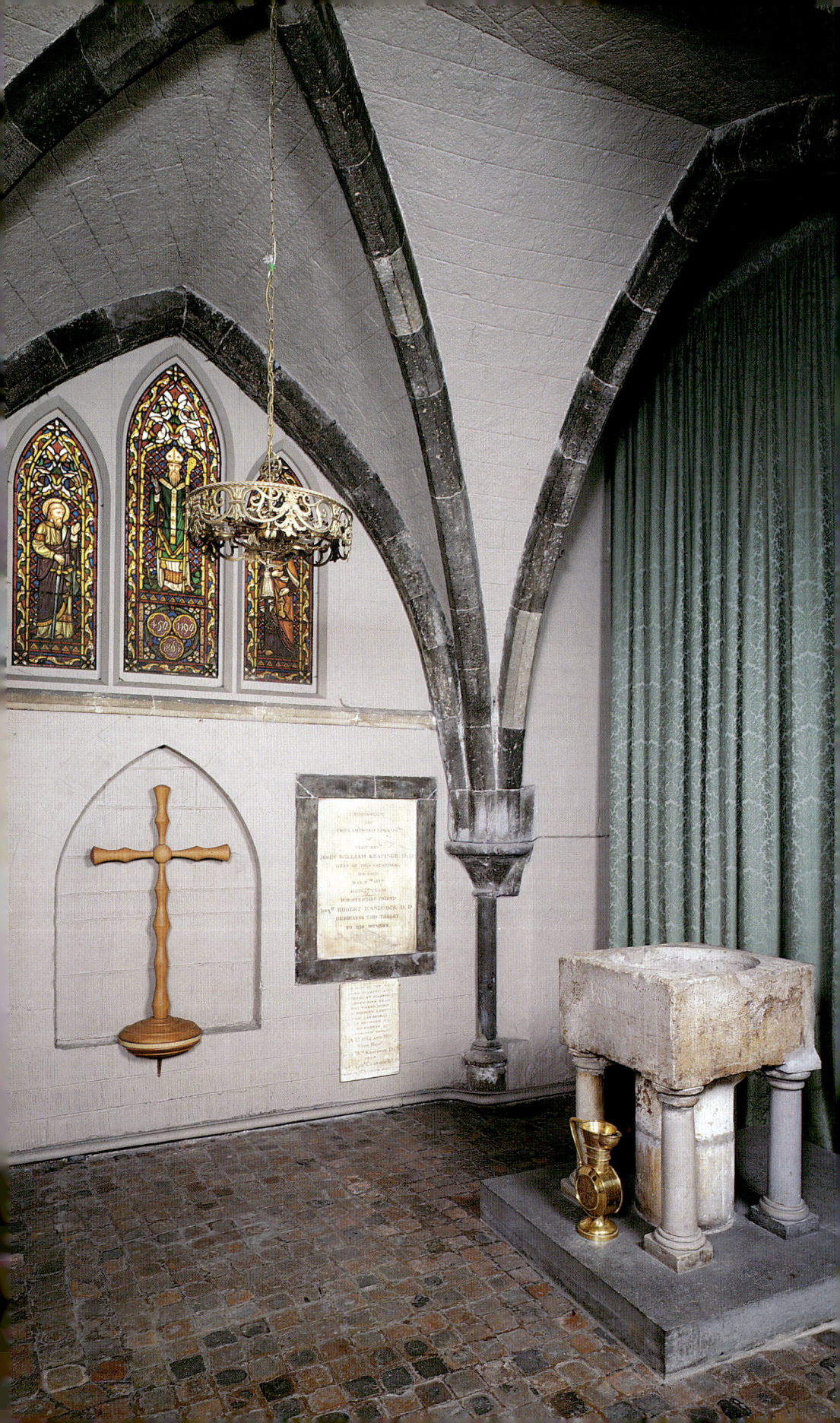